William Walton
A Song Album

Edited with an Introduction by
Christopher Palmer

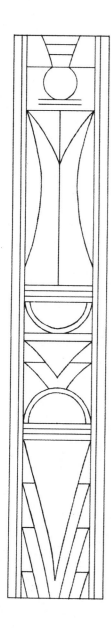

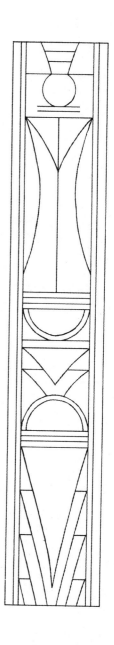

CONTENTS

INTRODUCTION

Until comparatively late in his career—his sixties, in fact—Walton took no more than a desultory interest in the solo song, despite the fact that both his parents were vocally gifted (his father was a singing teacher) and he himself had started his musical life as a choirboy at Christ Church, Oxford. The first two songs in this collection, 'The Winds' and 'Tritons', both date from the early 1920s and are among his first published works (J. Curwen & Sons Ltd. issued them both in 1921). Then in 1923 *Bucolic Comedies* appeared, five songs to words by Edith Sitwell. Three of these became the *Three Songs* of 1932, first performed by Hubert Foss (who founded the OUP Music Department) and his wife Dora. Two of the songs, 'Through Gilded Trellises' and 'Old Sir Faulk', are transcriptions (or rather recompositions) of familiar numbers from *Façade*. The first, 'Daphne', was also part of the original *Façade* but Walton eventually dropped it from the definitive version: he told Angus Morrison it had never been satisfactory in its spoken form and needed the singing voice. Because words take longer to enunciate when they are sung than when they are spoken, the tempi of these songs must in all cases depend on what is comfortable for the singer, and will inevitably be slower than in the spoken *Façade*. I suggest that 'Daphne' and 'Through Gilded Trellises' should be sung by a soprano, 'Old Sir Faulk' either by a soprano or tenor.

Despite his feeling for vocal colour and texture, Walton often treated voices like instruments, and his vocal melodic lines seem instrumentally conceived. (Conversely, and paradoxically, the *bel canto* quality of his melodic thought in instrumental contexts—the Violin Concerto, for example—has often been noted). Singers find *Anon. in Love* a difficult, though rewarding, piece to negotiate. We have now jumped forward nearly thirty years, to 1960. *Anon. in Love* was an Aldeburgh Festival commission, the dedicatees being Peter Pears (tenor) and Julian Bream (guitar). It was ironic that one of the first fruits of Walton's *rapprochement* with Benjamin Britten (relations between the two were uneasy in earlier days, as Britten gradually superseded Walton in the vanguard of English composers) should have been in the form of a solo song-cycle—a medium which Britten had virtually dominated for over twenty years. 1960 was the year of Britten's Shakespeare opera *A Midsummer Night's Dream*, to which the anonymous 16th- and 17th-century lyrics of *Anon. in Love* (texts from *The English Galaxy of Shorter Poems*, ed. Gerald Bullett, J. M. Dent and Sons Ltd.) provided a delightful complement. However, there is nothing at all Brittenish about the music: despite the centrality of Pears's voice, Walton resists the temptation to parody or even refer to Britten's vocal style, and Britten would have been too alienated by the innocent salaciousness of some of the texts ever to want to set them.

There was a Rabelaisian side to Walton's character, but he also had a patrician sensibility: he is saucy and mischievous at times in this music, but never uncouth. According to Frank Howes, the 'salacious' flavour of the last three songs belongs to the age of Purcell, and the similes and word-play of the first three are more typical of the Elizabethan period. The words of the first three songs are in fact familiar through their use by madrigal and lute composers. Graham Johnson has actually hailed Walton, on the basis of *Anon. in Love* (and of the somewhat later *A Song for the Lord Mayor's Table*) as a 'New Elizabethan'. There is nothing 'anonymous' about these songs, he suggests, apart from the authorship of the poems: it is the same 'incorrigibly passionate' Walton of old, 'but mellowed by a tender, even vulnerable lyricism. Like the erotic drawings of Picasso, these songs make up a portrait of a man rejuvenated in late middle-age by the hedonistic pleasures of new life and loves'.[1] Johnson goes on to describe the notion of a great Elizabethan writer of lute-songs serendipitously finding a 20th-century sunspot in which to take a holiday.

The age of those composers—when men like Thomas Campion, Robert Jones, and John Dowland wrote both words and music of their songs and then performed them themselves—seems impossibly remote today. All the more marvellous, then, is the freshness of *Anon. in Love*, which recreates the spirit of the Elizabethan age with miraculous spontaneity and with no hint of archaism or pastiche. Walton called on his old friend Christopher Hassall—poet, playwright, and librettist of his opera *Troilus and Cressida*—for professional help in the selection of texts. Hassall recognized that a contemporary age of what he called 'seen' poetry—argumentative, introspective, obscure poetry, meant not so much to be heard for its quality of sound (like Edith Sitwell's verse in *Façade*) as pored over on the page—spelt a bad time for the art of the song, or at least the type of song that a composer like Walton wanted to sing. So he turned instead to a time in which harmony between voice and verse was more ready-made. He knew his composer, and understood the virtues of plain and unpretentious verse as far as Walton was concerned. He divined also, I am sure, that a poem like 'Lady, when I behold the roses' might rekindle some of the great love-making ardour of Act II of *Troilus and Cressida*: has not the English rose always been a symbol of purity and flawless beauty, of all that is steadfastly unspoilt in a world of shifting values? Walton's setting is one of English music's most glorious love songs. The 'Elizabethanism' of *Anon. in Love* (there are odd glimpses of it in earlier Walton, mainly in the Shakespeare film scores), with its combination of sweetness and spicy, salty energy, recalls that of Peter Warlock, a composer not often mentioned in Walton's orbit, but greatly admired by him.

Pears and Bream recorded the original voice-and-guitar version of *Anon. in Love* (RCA RB 6621 [mono]; SB 6621 [stereo]), and in 1971 Walton arranged the accompaniment for strings, harp, and a touch of percussion (in the last two songs). I have drawn on both versions in making my piano transcription, which I hope will lead to more widespread performances. The pianist should bear in mind that the guitar's dynamic range is more limited than the piano's, and that the former's sonority is delicate and subtle. The *una corda* should be used freely, and nothing approaching a true *ff* reached until the end of the last song. When I have used the wedge staccato mark, the effect should be spiky rather than heavy. The repeated strummed chords in 'Fain would I change that note' should be played not rigidly but more in the fashion of an improvised accompaniment to the voice. This version was first performed by Martyn Hill (tenor) and Graham Johnson (piano) at a Songmakers' Almanack concert in the Wigmore Hall, London, 23 May 1989, and is published here for the first time.

It was the Worshipful Company of Goldsmiths (were they, I wonder, mindful of Walton's praising of the 'God of Gold' in *Belshazzar's Feast*?) who in 1962 charged the 'new Elizabethan' to deliver a song-cycle for voice and piano for the City of London Festival of that year. Walton again applied to Christopher Hassall, who made a choice of texts on aspects of London. Inscribed 'in Honour of the City' (a reference to Dunbar's *In Honour of the City of London* which Walton had set as a choral piece in 1937), *A Song for the Lord Mayor's Table* was given its first performance (in the Goldsmith's Hall) by Elisabeth Schwarzkopf and Gerald Moore in July 1962. Eight years later, in the Mansion House, at another City of London Festival concert, George Malcolm conducted the English Chamber Orchestra and Janet Baker in the first performance of the orchestral version.

The cycle requires a big, generous voice and a powerful vocal personality with a quasi-operatic flair for characterization. Walton never used the term 'symphonic' to describe the work, but he could have, for in many respects it applies: an 'important' first movement of broad design (A, B, recapitulation of A, coda); two contrasting intermezzi ('Glide Gently' and 'Wapping Old Stairs'); main slow movement ('Holy Thursday': Blake's poem describes the pathos of the annual service at St Paul's Cathedral on Ascension Day to which children from London's orphanages were marched two by two to give thanks for their scant blessings); main scherzo ('The Contrast'); and quicksilver finale based on the traditional tune 'Oranges and Lemons'. Frank Howes points out that the chopper of the child's singing-game ('Here comes a candle to light you to bed, And here comes a chopper to chop off your head') is missing here, since Walton sets a longer version from *Gammer Gurton's Garland* of 1810 in which there are many more bell-towers than in the nursery-rhyme version. 'Gay go up and gay go down' goes the 'old rhyme' which Walton sets in this finale, and his vision

[1] Programme note for a Songmakers' Almanack concert given at the Wigmore Hall, London, 23 May 1989.

(continued on p. 86)

THE WINDS

A. C. SWINBURNE
(1837–1909)

WILLIAM WALTON

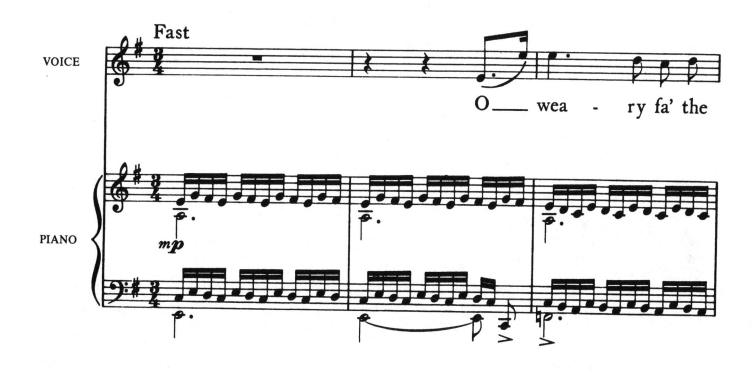

O— wea - ry fa' the east — wind,

And wea - ry fa' the

west: And gin I were un - - der the

wan_ waves wide_____ I wot weel_____ wad I

rest.   O___

wea - ry fa' the north___ wind, And

wea - ry fa' the south: The

sea went ower my good lord's head Or ev-er he kissed my

mouth.

Wea - ry fa' the wind - ward rocks, And

wea - ry fa' the lee: They

wea - ry fa' the sea: It might hae taken an hun - dred men, And let my ae love be.

TRITONS

W. DRUMMOND
(1585-1649)

WILLIAM WALTON

Nep - tune's li - quid plain, ____

When - ____ as ye shall ar - rive ____ With ____

tilt - ing tides where sil - ver O - ra

plays, And to your king his wa - t'ry tri - bute

a tempo

pays,

for Dora and Hubert Foss

DAPHNE

EDITH SITWELL
(1887-1964)

WILLIAM WALTON

11

flow - - ing locks, the king - - ly sun like a swain came strong, un-

- heeding of her scorn, Wad - ing in deeps where she___ has lain,___

Sleep - ing up - on___ her___ ri - - ver___ lawn And

chas - ing her star - ry sa - - tyr train. She fled, and changed in - to a

tree, that love - ly,_____ that love - - - - - ly, fair - haired_____

la - - dy_____ And_____ now I seek through the

sere_____ sum - - mer where no trees_____ are sha - - - dy!'_____

THROUGH GILDED TRELLISES

EDITH SITWELL
(1887-1964)

WILLIAM WALTON

Lento quasi improvissando ♩ = 88 c.

Allegretto grazioso ♪ = 176

sempre con rubato *p*

Through gild-ed

trel - li - ses of the heat, __ Do - lo - res, I - nez, Ma -

Through gild- ed trel - li - ses

of the heat,___ Spang - les pelt down through the___ tang - - les of___

bell flowers; Each

OLD SIR FAULK

EDITH SITWELL
(1887-1964)

WILLIAM WALTON

nurse-ry-maid Meg With a leg like a peg Chased the feath-ered dreams like hens, and

when they laid an egg in the sheep-skin meadows where,___ The___ se-

-rene King James would steer,___ Horse and hounds, then he From the

shade of a tree Picked it up as spoil to boil for nurse-ry

Pot and pan and cop - per ket - tle Put up -

- on their prop - er met - tle, Lest the Flood, the Flood, the

Flood be - gin a - gain through these, a - gain through these!

ANON. IN LOVE

Anon. 16th- and 17th-century lyrics,
selected by Christopher Hassall

WILLIAM WALTON
(Guitar part arranged for piano by
Christopher Palmer)

1. FAIN WOULD I CHANGE THAT NOTE

Lento amabile (♩ = c.88)   pp espress.

VOICE

Fain _____ would I change _ that note _____

PIANO

pp gently strummed (con 2 Ped.)

_ To which fond _____ Love _ hath charm'd _____ me, Long, _

long _ to sing _ by rote, Fan – cy-ing that_____ that_ harm'd

me: espr.   Yet when this thought doth come,   'Love is the per -fect

29

sum of all _____ de-light', _____ I have no oth-er

choice, Ei-ther for pen or voice _____ To sing _____

or write. _____

rit. _ _ _ _ _ _ _ molto p a tempo

O _ Love, _____ they wrong _ thee

2. O STAY, SWEET LOVE

3. LADY, WHEN I BEHOLD THE ROSES

Lady,— when I be - hold the ro - ses sprout - ing, Which clad in da-mask man - tles deck — the — ar - bours, And then be - hold your lips where sweet love — har - bours,— My eyes pre - sent me with a dou - ble — doubt — — —

4. MY LOVE IN HER ATTIRE

Allegro leggiero (♩ = c.116)

My Love in her at – tire doth show her wit, It

doth so well be – come her: For ev – ery sea – son she hath dress – ings

fit, For win – ter, spring, and sum – mer, win – ter, spring, for win – ter, spring, and

sum – mer. No beau – ty she doth miss When all her robes are

5. I GAVE HER CAKES AND I GAVE HER ALE

6. TO COUPLE IS A CUSTOM

[*CROWD = CRWTH, the forerunner of the viol, played with a bow.]

45

In honour of the City of London

A SONG FOR THE LORD MAYOR'S TABLE
1. THE LORD MAYOR'S TABLE

THOMAS JORDAN

WILLIAM WALTON

47

50

51

Strand,___ To pen, pen us a dit - ty in praise, praise of the

Ci - ty, Their trea - (ea)-sure and plea - (ea)-sure, their___

trea - sure, and plea-sure, their___ trea-sure, and___ plea-sure, their___

trea - sure, and plea-sure, To pen___ us a dit-ty in praise___

52

2. GLIDE GENTLY

glide, fair stream, for ev - er so, Thy qui - et soul on all bes-

-tow - ing, Till all our minds for ev - er flow As thy deep

wa - ters now___ are flow - ing,

now_____ are flow - ing.___

3. WAPPING OLD STAIRS

ANON.

WILLIAM WALTON

Your Mol-ly has nev-er been false, she de-clares, Since last time we part-ed at Wap-ping Old Stairs, When I swore that I still would con-tin-ue the same, And gave you the 'bac-co box, gave you the 'bac-co box, gave you the 'bac-co box

too,_____ I made._____ Though you threat-en'd, last Sun-day, to

walk in the Mall With Su-san from Dept-ford, and like-wise with Sal, In

si-lence I stood your un-kind-ness to hear, And on-ly up-braid-ed my

Tom,_____ up-braid-ed my Tom_____ with__

a tear:_____ Why should Sal, or should Su-san, than

4. HOLY THURSDAY

WILLIAM BLAKE
(1757-1827)

WILLIAM WALTON

thun-der-ings___ the seats__ of heaven a-mong: Be-neath them sit the

a-ged men, wise guard-ians of the poor. Then cher-ish, cher-ish

pi-ty,___ lest you drive_____ an an-gel from your

door.___

5. THE CONTRAST

CHARLES MORRIS

WILLIAM WALTON

But an ass on a com-mon, an ass on a com-mon, a goose,⸻ a goose on a green.

Your mag-pies and stock-doves may flirt a-mong trees, And cha-(a)-(a)-ter their trans-ports in

-cure, Where for one eye to kill, there's a thou - sand to

cresc.

cure. I know love's a dev-il, too

sub - tle to spy, That shoots through the soul, from the beam of an

eye; But in Lon - don these dev - ils so quick fly a - bout, That a

6. RHYME

ANON. 18th-CENTURY

WILLIAM WALTON

Gay___ go up and gay go down, To
ring___ the___ bells___ of Lon - don Town.___
Gay___ go up and gay go down, To

The vowels to be repeated. Ga-(a)y etc.

Old fa-ther bald-pate, Say the slow bells of Ald-gate.

You owe me ten shil-lings, Say the bells of St.

He-len's. When will you pay me? Say the bells of Old

Bai-ley. When I grow rich, Say the bells of Shore-

UNDER THE GREENWOOD TREE

WILLIAM SHAKESPEARE
(1564-1616)

WILLIAM WALTON

BEATRIZ'S SONG

(from *Christopher Columbus*)

LOUIS MACNEICE
(1907-63)

WILLIAM WALTON
(arr. Christopher Palmer)

Andante espressivo

When will he re- / -turn? On- ly to de- part. Har- rowed by the o - men Of his rest - less heart; Bonds - man of the voice,

Printed and bound in Great Britain by
Caligraving Limited Thetford Norfolk

of London duly encompasses both high-life and low. There is real London pride-and-joy about 'The Lord Mayor's Table' (of an unexpectedly non-pomp-and-circumstantial kind!), and it is one of Walton's sturdiest tunes. Then Wordsworth's calm vista of the Thames is evoked: grey-blue sonority, grey-blue key (B flat). This and the flashing, kaleidoscopic brilliance of 'Rhyme', a study not just in rhyme and varied on-going repetition but also in bell-sonorities (Edith Sitwell would have applauded), remind us that as a magician in sound alone Walton has sovereign status. The racy Lancastrian (a bit like Shakespeare's Pistol) peeps out of 'Wapping Old Stairs'; and it is impossible not to hear in 'The Contrast' an ironic autobiographical *cri de coeur*. Note the yawning, punning reference to 'composing', which recalls Walton's remark (to Tony Palmer) to the effect that once mewed up in his island fastness on Ischia he composed primarily because there was nothing else to do. The coda, one of Walton's funniest inventions, seemingly looks back to those pre-war, high-society London days when 'devils' (in female guise) were in plentiful supply.

'Under the Greenwood Tree' and 'Beatriz's Song' stand outside the chronology of Walton's art-songs. The former—a clever pastiche of Morley and Dowland, with a piano part suggesting a lute—was written for (but not used in) the 1936 film *As You Like It*. 'Beatriz's Song' comes from *Christopher Columbus*, a radio play by Louis MacNeice, produced in 1942, for which Walton provided incidental music; the accompaniment was originally scored for strings and should therefore be played as smoothly and gently as possible.

CHRISTOPHER PALMER
London, June 1990